THE ELEMENTS IN POETRY

FIRE

KU-471-117

First published in paperback in 2010 by Evans Brothers Limited

2A Portman Mansions

Chiltern St

London W1U 6NR

All rights reserved. No part of this publication may be reproduced, stored in a retrieval system or transmitted in any form,
or by any means, electronic, mechanical, photocopying,
recording or otherwise, without the prior permission of Evans
Brothers Limited.

© Evans Brothers Limited 2007

British Library Cataloguing in Publication Data
Fire. - (The elements of poetry)
    1. Fire - Juvenile poetry
    I. Peters, Andrew (Andrew Fusek)
    808.8'1936

ISBN: 978 0237527785

Editorial: Julia Bird & Su Swallow
Design: Simon Borrough
Production: Jenny Mulvanny

CONTENTS

RED ALERT Graham Denton   6

WHY SANTA CLAUS SOMETIMES PREFERS THE FRONT DOOR
   J Patrick Lewis   6

LIGHT THE FESTIVE CANDLES (FOR HANUKKAH)
   Aileen Fisher   7

DIWALI – FESTIVAL OF LIGHT Jim Hatfield   8

HOT HEAD Philip Waddell   9

EXTRACT FROM THE DIARY OF THOMAS FARYNOR Steve Fisher   9

THE GREAT FIRE Eric Finney   10

GUY FORKS Andrew Fusek Peters   12

AUTUMN FIRES Robert Louis Stevenson   13

THE SONG OF THE STARS From a Pasmaquoddy Indian Song   13

CORROBOREE Oodgeroo Noonuccal   14

LOOKING INTO A FIRE Jim Hatfield   15

THE SUN Penny Kent   16

MY PET FIRE Clare Kirwan   17

A BONFIRE Gerard Benson   18

FLAME George Szirtes   19

VOLCANO TRIOLET Alison Chisholm   20

HANG-GLIDING OVER ACTIVE VOLCANOES Brian Moses   21

TELL ME TIGER Clare Bevan   22

AN EXTRACT FROM ANNUS MIRABILIS - 1666
   John Dryden   23

THE FLIGHT OF ICARUS J Patrick Lewis   24

SUNSET AT WIDEMOUTH BAY Wendy Cope   24

PROMETHEUS Paul Francis   25

THE CANDLE Andrew Fusek Peters   26

JANUARY – AN EXCERPT FROM THE SHEPHERD'S CALENDAR
   John Clare   27

RED ALERT

It's a...

Sun-dweller
Gas-brother
Fast-burner
Match-lover
Wet-hater
Flame-thrower
Coal-licker
Smoke-blower
Dark-splitter
Hearth-baker
Spark-spitter
Ash-maker
Wax-melter
Wood-torcher
Ice-breaker
Skin-scorcher
Paint-peeler
Hot-header
Fate-sealer
Quick-spreader

FIRE!

GRAHAM DENTON

Why Santa Claus Sometimes Prefers the Front Door

He remembers
Those Decembers
Burning embers
Chimney holes,

When he splendid-
Ly descended,
But rear-ended...
On the coals!

J Patrick Lewis

LIGHT THE FESTIVE CANDLES {FOR HANUKKAH}

Light the first of eight tonight –
the furthest candle to the right.

Light the first and second, too,
when tomorrow's day is through.

Then light three, and then light four –
every dusk one candle more

Till all eight burn bright and high,
honouring a day gone by

When the Temple was restored,
rescued from the Syrian lord,

And an eight-day feast proclaimed –
The Festival of Lights – well named

To celebrate the joyous day
when we regained the right to pray
to our one God in our own way.

Aileen Fisher

7

Diwali - Festival of Light

Narak has been
Put to flight
By Krishna in their
Godly fight.

Rama, defeating
Wrong with right
Was guided home
By candle-light.

My house is scrubbed
And painted bright.
Will Lakshmi visit
Me tonight?

Jim Hatfield

HOT HEAD

Touchy match,
Cap of red,
Had an itch
On its head.

Didn't think,
Foolish match,
Didn't think –
Had a scratch!

Philip Waddell

EXTRACT FROM THE DIARY OF THOMAS FARYNOR

BAKER TO KING CHARLES II, PUDDING LANE, LONDON

Sunday September 2nd 1666

12.30 am and I've just got home from work, made 300 loaves today plus a dozen doughnuts {with pink icing on top} for the king. They're his favourites!

Really tired, going to bed now, got an early start tomorrow.

Keep thinking I've forgotten to do something...
Did I turn the oven off?

Ah well, what's the worst that can happen?

STEVE FISHER

THE GREAT FIRE

London: sixteen sixty six;
In the dead of night a small flame licks…
From a bakery in Pudding Lane
A flicker first then a burst of flame.
A house, then a street of houses ablaze,
Fire funnels the narrow passageways
And fanned by wind it quickly spreads.
Londoners scramble from their beds.
After a summer parched with drought
Wooden buildings are all dried out:
On them the fire leaps greedily
And fear and panic now run free.
Loaded carts in crowded streets
Are piled with tables, chairs, beds, sheets:
To salvage something people try –
"Head for the river!" comes the cry
And on the Thames is soon afloat
Anything that will serve as a boat.

Now all the City is aflame,
No fire-fighting worth the name.
King Charles, attired in his nightgown,
Commands the speedy pulling down
Of buildings in the fire's way:
This done, the inferno loses sway,
With nothing left to feed upon
It gradually subsides, is gone.

Fire, it's said, cleans and purifies
And though in ashes London lies
The deadly poisons left alive
From the Black Death in sixty five
Are burned away. Small comfort this
To ease the sense of hopelessness
Of citizens whose homes burned down –
Thousands such in London Town.
St Pauls has gone, the Guildhall too:
Londoners have much to do.
The City must be built anew.

*[Want to know more? You'll find heaps
In the Diary of Mr Samuel Pepys]*

ERIC FINNEY

Guy Forks

The hill above London Town
Is filled with a feast of light,
Catherine Wheels are Wagon Wheels
Spinning like sweets in the night.

Sparklers dance their sherbert fizz,
Blown out by the wind so sour,
Rockets leap like liquorice lace,
And explode in a sugar shower.

Bangers go plop in a mushy mash,
The flames are eating the Guy,
Chestnuts tap-dance on the coals,
And taste like heaven! I sigh.

Hot dogs warm as the bonfire,
With mustard sharp as the cold,
November the fifth is a feast,
For this hungry eight year old!

Andrew Fusek Peters

AUTUMN FIRES

In the other gardens
And all up the vale,
From the autumn bonfires
See the smoke trail!

Pleasant summer over
And all the summer flowers,
The red fire blazes,
The grey smoke towers.

Sing a song of seasons!
Something bright in all!
Flowers in the summer,
Fires in the fall!

ROBERT LOUIS STEVENSON

The Song of the Stars

We are the stars which sing.
We sing with our light.
We are the birds of fire
We fly across the heavens.

From a Passamaquoddy Indian Song

Corroboree

Hot day dies, cook time comes.
Now between the sunset and sleeptime
Time of playabout.
  The hunters paint black bodies by firelight with
    Designs of meaning
      To dance corroboree.
        Now didgeridoo compels with haunting drone
        Eager feet to stamp,
      Click-sticks click in rhythm to swaying bodies
      Dancing corroboree.
  Like spirit things in from the great surrounding dark
              Ghost-gums dimly seen stand at the edge of the light
                Watching corroboree.
                  Eerie the scene in the leaping firelight,
                    Eerie the sounds in that wild setting
                      As naked dancers weave stories of the tribe
                        Into corroboree.

Oodgeroo Noonuccal

Looking into a Fire

Long
Ago when
The coal in this
Grate was a tree;
The sun shone upon its
Leaves and they held
Tight hold of that
Light for more years
Than you might ever
Count. Tonight,
Looking into the
Crimson glow,
We can feel
The sunlight
Breaking
Free
As
The
Tree
Lets
Go.

Jim Hatfield

THE SUN

Our
Earth would fit a
Million times inside the
Giant sun;   ball of burning
Gases giving light to everyone.
The sun's a star that pulls the
Planets round and round and
Round, by gravity, the force that
Holds us firmly to the ground.
Without the sun there'd be no
Life, no creatures, grass or
Trees. We need the
Sun - without its heat
Everything would
Freeze.

PENNY KENT

My Pet Fire

I was in my room at dead of night
And thought I'd make a little light,
So I struck a match, watched it ignite
My pet fire, burning bright.

Oh he was slender, gentle, slight
Orange and red, such a delight!
And everything was quite alright
With my pet fire, burning bright.

And though I thought I held him tight
In just a flash, he took a bite
And I let go in such a fright
Of my pet fire, burning bright.

He grew up to an awful height,
Was glowing red - a terrible sight
And reached an enormous Fahrenheit:
My pet fire, burning bright.

I coud feel its heat, its might
And no-one knew my dreadful plight,
It was too big - I couldn't fight
My pet fire, burning bright.

I'm still smoldering as I write
My house is black, my scars are white.
If you want to play, please don't invite
My pet fire, burning bright.

Clare Kirwan

A BONFIRE

A poem is a bonfire,
Difficult to get going,
But once lit it will rage,
Rage and burn.

It is beautiful to look at,
Golden orange,
But beware! It can hurt you.
Stand clear. Handle with care.

You can feed it on anything -
Old sticks and twigs of ideas -
First drafts. Once it is going
Nothing will be beyond it.

If it's a good one
You can gather round it
With songs, stories,
Or deeply felt ideas.

Leave it for a time
And then come back to it.
Is it still warm?
Does smoke still rise?

GERARD BENSON

18

FLAME

Fire
Multiplies
Fire makes fire
A whole leaping choir
Fire wider and higher
Watching the sparks fly
Watching smoke rise
Each hiss and flicker
A spreadable snicker
But there, there
Without air
Fire dies
No spark
Just dark
Wick
Stick
Thick
Dark

Gone

GEORGE SZIRTES

Volcano Triolet

A cloud of dust and ash explodes;
The mountain vomits jets of fire
While churning magma boils and flows.
A cloud of dust and ash explodes,
And lava surges blazing roads
Down routes where earth and hell conspire.
A cloud of dust and ash explodes;
The mountain vomits jets of fire.

Alison Chisholm

HANG-GLIDING OVER ACTIVE VOLCANOES

It was truly amazing the first time I dared
Like surfin' in a furnace, but wow, was I scared!
That first time I tried it, I nearly died,
Grilled to perfection on the underside.

Yes, I got singed from my eyebrows to my toes,
From hang-gliding over active volcanoes.

I saw bubbling lava, fountains of fire,
Felt warm blasts lifting me even higher.
I was floating along on waves of steam
While applying layers of suntan cream.

Yes, I got singed from my eyebrows to my toes,
From hang-gliding over active volcanoes.

And it didn't take long to get me really hooked
On that great sensation of feeling half-cooked.
What a thrill, I could chill in this situation
If I don't succumb to asphyxiation.

Yes, I got singed from my eyebrows to my toes,
I got scorched from my kneecaps to my nose
From hang-gliding over active volcanoes.

BRIAN MOSES

TELL ME TIGER

After William Blake

Tell me tiger,
What became
Of your stripes as bright
As a jungle flame?

What became of
Your glittering eyes
Sharp as stars
In the jungle skies?

What became of
Your flickering tail
Curved and coiled
As a jungle trail?

What became of
Your fiery heart
When the jungle patterns
Ripped apart?

When the jungle smoke
Swirled ghostly blue,
Tiger, what became
Of you?

Clare Bevan

AN EXTRACT FROM
ANNUS MIRABILIS 1666

Such was the rise of this prodigious fire,
Which in mean buildings first obscurely bred,
From thence did soon to open streets aspire,
And straight to palaces and temples spread.

In this deep quiet, from what source unknown,
Those seeds of fire their fatal birth disclose:
And first, few scattering sparks about were blown,
Big with the flames that to our ruin rose.

Then, in some close-pent room it crept along,
And, smouldering as it went, in silence fed;
Till the infant monster, with devouring strong,
Walk'd boldly upright with exalted head.

JOHN DRYDEN

The Flight of Icarus

I rose on wings of wax,
Tracing angel tracks.

The sun called out my name
And I took reckless aim

Upward - the chosen one
First to kiss the Sun!

I started to perspire
In universal fire,

As if God struck a match
And somehow I could catch

Its light and hold it long…
I was wrong.

J Patrick Lewis

SUNSET AT WIDEMOUTH BAY

Fire,
Behind the sea
The sky is full of long-winged angels,
Burning.

WENDY COPE

PROMETHEUS

Prometheus, the Titan, walks through heaven
Burning to let man learn; this warm desire
Ignites his future hopes, once men are given
What only gods possess, the gift of fire.

"It cannot be. Your pity does you proud
but think what they will do with it, these men,
a weak, short-sighted, violent crowd,"
said Zeus. "The answer's no. Don't ask again."

He didn't ask. He took a tiny spark,
Hid in a little tube of wood, and raced
Down from Olympus, earthbound through the dark.
He could not see what followed - blazing huts,
The bombs, the torture, and the life he faced
Chained to a rock as an eagle gnawed his guts.

Paul Francis

THE CANDLE

Three in one and one in three
This candle is a trinity.

One for the darkness
Filled with doubt,
Will we ever
Put it out?

Two for the light
So bright and pure
Pray it shall be
Shadow's cure.

Three for the flickering
hope we see
That leads at last
To trinity.

Three in one and one in three
This candle is a trinity.

ANDREW FUSEK PETERS

JANUARY - EXCERPT FROM THE SHEPHERD'S CALENDAR 1827

A Cottage evening

The shutters closd the lamp alight
The faggot chopt and blazing bright
The shepherd from his labour free
Dancing his childern on his knee
Or toasting sloe boughs sputtering ripe
Or smoaking glad his puthering pipe
While underneath his masters seat
The tird dog lies in slumbers sweet
Startling and whimpering in his sleep
Chasing still the straying sheep
The cat rolld round in vacant chair
Or leaping childerns knees to lair
Or purring on the warmer hearth
Sweet chorus to the crickets mirth
The redcap hanging overhead
In cage of wire is perchd abed
Slumbering in his painted feathers
Unconcous of the outdoor weathers
And things wi out the cottage walls
Meet comfort as the evening falls
As happy in the winters dearth
As those around the blazing hearth

JOHN CLARE

Author Index

Gerard Benson
A Bonfire 18

Clare Bevan
Tell Me Tiger 22

Alison Chisholm
Volcano Triolet 20

John Clare
January – Excerpt from the 27
Shepherd's Calendar

Wendy Cope
Sunset at Widemouth Bay 24

Graham Denton
Red Alert 6

John Dryden
An Extract From Annus Mirabilis 23
1666

Eric Finney
The Great Fire 10

Aileen Fisher
Light the Festive Candles 7
(for Hanukkah)

Steve Fisher
Extract from the Diary of 9
Thomas Farynor

Paul Francis
Prometheus 25

Jim Hatfield
Diwali – Festival of Light 8
Looking into a Fire 15

Penny Kent
The Sun 16

Clare Kirwan
My Pet Fire 17

J Patrick Lewis
Why Santa Claus Sometimes 6
Prefers the Front Door
The Flight of Icarus 24

Brian Moses
Hang-Gliding Over Active 21
Volcanoes

Oodgeroo Noonuccal
Corroboree 14

Pasmaquoddy
Song of the Stars 13

Andrew Fusek Peters
Guy Forks 12
The Candle 26

Robert Louis Stevenson
Autumn Fires 13

George Szirtes
Flame 19

Philip Waddell
Hot Head 9

ACKNOWLEDGEMENTS

Gerard Benson: 'A Bonfire', by permission of the author.
Clare Bevan: 'Tell Me Tiger', by permission of the author.
Alison Chisholm: 'Volcano Triolet', by permission of the author.
Wendy Cope: 'Sunset at Widemouth Bay', with the author's permission.
Graham Denton: 'Red Alert', by permission of the author.
Eric Finney: 'The Great Fire', © Eric Finney. By permission of the author.
Steve Fisher: 'Extract from the Diary of Thomas Farynor', by permission of the author.
Paul Francis: 'Prometheus', by permission of the author.
Jim Hatfield: 'Diwali – Festival of Light' and 'Looking into a Fire', by permission of the author.
Penny Kent: 'The Sun' © Penny Kent 2006. By permission of the author.
Clare Kirwan: 'My Pet Fire', by permission of the author.
J. Patrick Lewis: 'The Flight of Icarus' copyright © J. Patrick Lewis. Reprinted by permission of Curtis Brown, Ltd.
Oodgeroo Noonuccal: 'Corroboree' by Oodgeroo of the tribe Noonuccal, from *My People*, 3e, The Jacaranda Press, 1990, Reproduced by permission of John Wiley & Sons Australia
Andrew Fusek Peters: 'Guy Forks' and 'The Candle', © Andrew Fusek Peters. By permission of the author.
Philip Waddell: 'Hot Head', by permission of the author.

Every effort has been made to trace the copyright holders, but in some cases this has not proved possible. The publisher will be happy to rectify any such errors or omissions in future reprints and/or new editions.

PICTURE CREDITS

Cover: © Catherine Karnow/Corbis
p.7: istockphoto © Charles Shapiro
p.8: © Manjunath Kiran/epa/Corbis
p.9: istockphoto © David Freund
p.10 & 11: The Great Fire of London in 1666 (oil on canvas), Verschuier, Lieve (1630-86)/Museum of Fine Arts, Budapest, Hungary,/The Bridgeman Art Library
p.12: © Adrian Carroll; eye ubiquitous/Corbis
p.13: NASA
p.14: © Ralph A. Clevenger/Corbis
p.16: © Larry Lee Photography/Corbis
p.17: © Josh Westrich/zefa/Corbis
p.18: © Ashley Cooper/Corbis
p.20: © Kevin Schafer/Corbis
p.22: istockphoto
p.23: © Bettmann/Corbis
p.24 & 25: istockphoto © John Chang
p.27: istockphoto
p.28: © Simon Borrough

THE ELEMENTS IN POETRY

Poems from the other books in this series

BLUEBOTTLE

Who dips, dives,
swoops out of space,
a buzz in his wings
and sky on his face;
now caught in the light,
now gone without trace,
a sliver of glass,
never still in one place?

Who's elusive as a pickpocket,
lord of the flies;
who moves like a rocket,
bound for the skies?
Who's catapult, aeroplane,
always full-throttle?
Sky-diver, Jumping Jack,
comet,
bluebottle!

Judith Nicholls

Taken from **Air**
ISBN 978 0 237 52781 5

Rain in the City

I had only known the splash
and the pelt and the scatter,
the gush and the gurgle of gutters
and the tumbled drums of the thunder –
until I looked downwards from an upstairs
office-block
and saw the sudden flowering
of a thousand umbrellas
in a most unlikely spring.

Anne Bell

Taken from **Water**
ISBN 978 0 237 52779 2

THE GOOD EARTH

More precious than gold,
Some call it mud
But earth makes bodies
Bone and blood.
It grows the plants
Which feed us all
So, birds and beasts,
Both large and small
Come from earth
As humans do.
Earth has grown
Me and you.
More precious than gold,
Don't call it mud,
Call it bodies,
Bone and blood.

Marian Swinger

Taken from **Earth**
ISBN 978 0 237 52780 8

About the anthologist

Andrew Fusek Peters, together with his wife Polly, has written and edited over 45 books for young people. Their last two verse collections were nominated for the Carnegie Medal and his poems have been recorded for the Poetry Archive (www.poetryarchive.org). His collection Mad, Bad & Dangerously Haddock features the best of his poetry for children over the last 20 years and his anthology Sheep Don't Go To School has been recommended by QCA as part of their Reading Differences scheme. Out of Order, his last anthology for the Evans Publishing Group, was highly praised.

"...an experienced and accomplished anthologist" TES

"His anthologies are always surprising and interesting. He's done it again..." Books for Keeps five star review.

Andrew is also an experienced schools' performer, quite a good juggler and mean didgeridoo player. Check him out on www.tallpoet.com.